CW01188894

THE UNITED NATIONS

The Organisation at the
Heart of International Diplomacy

Written by Camille David
In collaboration with Thomas Jacquemin
Translated by Rebecca Neal

History **50MINUTES.com**

50MINUTES.com

BECOME AN EXPERT
IN HISTORY

George Washington

The Battle of Austerlitz

Neil Armstrong

The Six-Day War

The Fall of Constantinople

www.50minutes.com

THE UNITED NATIONS 9

Key information
Introduction

POLITICAL, SOCIAL AND ECONOMIC CONTEXT 13

The League of Nations (1919-1946): the forerunner of the United Nations

The interwar period, or the failure of peace

The Second World War and the desire for a new organisation

BIOGRAPHY 21

Franklin D. Roosevelt, American president

THE CREATION OF THE UNITED NATIONS 25

From plan to reality

The Charter of the United Nations

IMPACT 41

International peace and security

Disarmament and nuclear control

Support for economic wellbeing and cooperation

Support for social wellbeing and cooperation

A world without the UN

SUMMARY 55

FIND OUT MORE 61

THE UNITED NATIONS

KEY INFORMATION

- **Date founded:** 24 October 1945 (ratification of the Charter of the United Nations).
- **Headquarters:** New York City.
- **Key protagonist:** Franklin D. Roosevelt, American president (1882-1945).
- **Impact:**
    - Establishment of peacekeeping operations
    - Control of nuclear power
    - Support for economic and social welfare

INTRODUCTION

The United Nations (UN) is a key player on the international stage and is often in the spotlight. It carries out countless activities throughout the world, including mediation in peace negotiations, peacekeeping through the Blue Berets, humanitarian aid in countries hit by natural disasters, and the coordination of medical aid during epidemics. However, the organisation does not always receive good press, and has been criticised for its inability to resolve certain conflicts and for its structure, which is deemed outdated and poorly equipped to address current realities and challenges. Indeed, its harshest critics have even questioned whether the UN should still exist.

The UN is the successor to the League of Nations (founded in 1919) and is not a recent organisation: it was founded in the aftermath of the ravages of the Second World War (1939-1945) and was inspired by the desire to create a better world. It was officially founded on 24 October 1945, when the Charter of the United Nations entered into force. Its aim was to provide a space for political dialogue between member states and in this way to prevent the outbreak of another war and resolve the many problems caused by the global conflict. Its structure and functioning reflected the new postwar world order. The creation of the UN had far-reaching consequences, and even today many other bodies depend on the organisation. With the end of the Cold War and the emergence of new challenges for humanity, the scope of its activities is constantly expanding, but some still wonder whether the organisation truly belongs in the modern world.

POLITICAL, SOCIAL AND ECONOMIC CONTEXT

THE LEAGUE OF NATIONS (1919-1946): THE FORERUNNER OF THE UNITED NATIONS

The United Nations was not the first international organisation with a broad jurisdiction to be created in the 20th century. It was preceded by the League of Nations, which was founded in 1919 in the wake of the First World War.

The idea for the League of Nations was put forward by Woodrow Wilson (1856-1924), the American president during the war. His "Fourteen Points" (a series of principles designed to guide the peace process) included the creation of a global body tasked with maintaining peace so that the horrors of the Great War would never be repeated. The Covenant of the League of Nations was signed by 42 founding members, the majority of which had participated in the conflict.

The Covenant set out the organisation's three main objectives:

- to prevent wars based on the principle of collective security;
- to enforce international law through the creation of a Permanent Court of International Justice in 1922, and to resolve disputes through negotiation and mediation;
- to improve citizens' overall quality of life.

The League of Nations was run by a General Assembly with representatives from all the member states, a Council comprising nine members (five of which were permanent, namely Great Britain, the USA, France, Italy and Japan, and four of which were non-permanent and elected by the General Assembly), and a Secretariat tasked with the administrative management of the organisation.

Did you know?

The League of Nations marked a major shift in the philosophy of diplomacy, as it aimed to replace secret diplomacy with collective negotiation. Previously, international relations were governed by treaties, diplomatic missions and conferences, but there was often no continuity between them. Wilson's goal was therefore to create a permanent organisation tasked with defusing tensions on an international level. This laid the foundations for the new principle of collective security, whereby each country acknowledged that its security could affect the security of the other nations, and vice versa. The countries therefore agreed to coordinate a joint response to threats and infractions affecting one of them. The principle of collective action meant that each country had to be ready to react swiftly to take up arms and defend another country.

THE INTERWAR PERIOD, OR THE FAILURE OF PEACE

The idea behind the League of Nations was bold and represented a new outlook on diplomatic relations, but the organisation was ultimately a failure. In September 1939, Nazi Germany and the USSR invaded Poland, plunging the world into the Second World War. The League of

Nations had failed in its peacekeeping role: it had proved unable to stop the rise of Nazism and to put a stop to the aggression of the Axis countries (Germany, Italy and Japan) in the interwar period.

There were multiple reasons for this failure. Firstly, the League of Nations did not have its own army and therefore relied on the goodwill of the major world powers to enforce its decisions. The organisation's moral authority alone was not enough to force individual members to comply with its orders. Secondly, not all countries joined the League of Nations. Notable absences included the USA (which had been the driving force behind the creation of the organisation) and the USSR, which did not join until 1934. Without these two key powers, the defence of the League of Nations' principles fell to Great Britain and France, which were both following a policy of appeasement and were reluctant to impose their will by force. Furthermore, since membership was not an essential condition to play an important role on the international stage, it was easy for countries to join and leave the League of Nations as they pleased without becoming pariahs. Consequently, certain powerful countries decided to simply leave the organisation when it tried to check their nationalist, expansionist aspirations: Japan and Germany withdrew in 1933, and Italy followed suit in 1937.

THE SECOND WORLD WAR AND THE DESIRE FOR A NEW ORGANISATION

The outbreak of war in 1939 sounded the death knell for the League of Nations, but as early as 1941, when Europe was almost entirely under the yoke of the Axis powers, some countries were already thinking ahead to the end of the war and making plans for the creation of a new institution. The human and material destruction wreaked by the war underlined the need for political dialogue between countries once peace was restored. To this end, a number of countries began taking steps to prepare the way for the new organisation from the early stages of the war:

- On 12 June 1941, the **Declaration of St. James's Palace** was signed by nine governments in exile in London (Belgium, Czechoslovakia, Free France, Greece, Luxembourg, the Netherlands, Norway, Poland and Yugoslavia). The signatories committed to working with other free peoples in wartime and peacetime, and in doing so laid the foundations of the UN.

- On 14 August 1941, the **Atlantic Charter** was ratified. Before the USA entered the conflict, the American president Franklin D. Roosevelt and the British prime minister Winston Churchill (1874-1965) signed a joint declaration (known as the Atlantic Charter because it was signed in a ship on the ocean) affirming their intention to create a new institution for peacekeeping and international security. Their plan outlined some of the organising principles of the postwar period, such as freedom of the seas, disarmament and the establishment of an international court of justice.
- On 1 January 1942, **the Declaration of the United Nations** was signed. At a time when the majority of Europe was occupied by German forces, representatives from 26 nations fighting the Axis countries signed a joint declaration of their total commitment to the war effort and their refusal to accept any peace agreement with the enemy. This was the first time the expression "United Nations" was used.

- At the **Moscow Conference** in October 1943 and the **Tehran Conference** in December 1943, the four major Allied powers (the USSR, Great Britain, the USA and China) reaffirmed their desire to create an international body tasked with peacefully resolving conflicts as soon as possible after the end of the war.

At the end of the conflict, the international community found itself facing a host of other problems, including the refugee situation, the fate of deportees, orphans and the wounded, sanitary issues and epidemics. In addition, a new war remained a looming possibility. In this context, an international organisation to coordinate the activities of all the bodies created during the war became a necessity.

BIOGRAPHY

FRANKLIN D. ROOSEVELT, AMERICAN PRESIDENT

Portrait of Franklin D. Roosevelt, dated 1933.

Franklin Roosevelt was the 32nd president of the United States, and led the country from 1933 to his death in 1945. He was one of the towering figures of the 20th century, and remains one of the USA's most celebrated presidents.

He was born in Hyde Park in the state of New York on 30 January 1882, and was the only son of a wealthy businessman. He graduated from Harvard University with a law degree in 1904, and before long entered politics and was elected senator for New York, representing the Democratic Party. In spite of an illness which left him partially paralysed, he went on to become governor of the state of New York, before being elected president in 1932.

When he came to power, the country was still reeling from the effects of the Wall Street Crash in 1929. He immediately implemented emergency measures, and starting in 1933 introduced the New Deal, a collection of programmes based on far-reaching government intervention in the economy and in social matters. Having set the country on the path to recovery, he was re-elected for a second term in 1936 and a third term in 1940.

Although the USA did not enter the war against Germany until December 1941, Roosevelt backed the Western democracies by providing them with financial and logistical support in their fight against the Axis countries. He was a firm believer in the need for an international organisation to maintain peace through collective action, and was one of the driving forces behind the Atlantic Charter, which paved the way for the United Nations. He was also the first person to use the term "United Nations" in the eponymous declaration, and played a major role in shaping the postwar world order.

He died on 12 April 1945, shortly after the beginning of his fourth term as president and only a few days before the conference to draw up the Charter of the United Nations in San Francisco. He left his country in a strong position as the world's leading economy and the foremost defender of democracy at the dawn of the Cold War.

THE CREATION OF THE UNITED NATIONS

FROM PLAN TO REALITY

The first real step towards the creation of the UN was the Dumbarton Oaks Conference near Washington from 21 August to 7 October 1944. This brought together representatives from the USA, the USSR, Great Britain and China to lay the groundwork for the nascent organisation, specifically by discussing its general objectives, structure and functioning. After the conference, the various members of the United Nations had the opportunity to look over the resulting proposals and give their feedback and suggestions.

The conference ended in disagreement over the crucial issue of the conditions for joining the organisation and securing the right to vote. The USSR wanted all its constituent republics to have the right to vote, which would have given the country several votes. The USA could not accept this, and this disagreement foreshadowed the coming rift between the USA and the USSR.

The matter was settled during the Yalta Conference in February 1945, which brought together the leaders of the USA, the USSR and Great Britain. This meeting finished the work that had been started at the Dumbarton Oaks Conference and resulted in a partial agreement concerning the number of Soviet republics that could become UN member states: the Byelorussian Soviet Socialist Republic and the Ukrainian Soviet Socialist Republic would each have a vote, taking the USSR's total number of votes to three.

THE CHARTER OF THE UNITED NATIONS

The United Nations Conference on International Organization (25 April to 26 June 1945)

The next conference to draw up the Charter of the United Nations took place in San Francisco and 45 countries were invited. The unexpected death of the US president Roosevelt gave rise to fears that the event would be cancelled, but his successor Harry S. Truman (1884-1972) decided to continue as planned. Consequently, delegates from 50 countries descended on San Francisco from 25 April to 26 June to take part in this historic conference.

> **DID YOU KNOW?**
>
> 45 countries received the invitation sent on 5 March 1945, but 50 countries were in attendance and there are 51 signatures on the Charter. Why is this?
>
> The 45 invitees were the countries that had declared war on Germany and Japan, and had therefore signed the Declaration of the United Nations. They were joined by Libya and Syria, which were invited by France, the two Soviet republics of the Ukraine and Byelorussia, and Argentina and Denmark, which had just been liberated, taking the total number of participants to 51. However, Poland was unable to attend the conference as its new government was not announced in time. Space was left on the Charter so that it could sign later on and become one of the organisation's 51 founding members. There are currently 193 UN

> member states, representing almost all the countries of the world, with the exception of four states that are recognised but are not members, namely Palestine, Vatican City, the Cook Islands and Niue (an island in the South Pacific Ocean). As statehood is one of the conditions for membership, territories such as Kosovo and Tibet, which are not recognised by all member states, cannot join the organisation.

Getting 50 countries to agree on the document's content was no mean feat. Differences of opinion resulted in a series of crises that led some observers to fear that there would be no agreement at the end of the conference. For example, the issue of the trusteeship of the former colonies of the defeated countries and the question of the great powers' right to veto were bumps in the road. However, these disagreements were eventually resolved and the Charter was adopted by unanimous agreement on 25 June 1945. It was signed by delegates from each of the 50 states the following day, but did not enter into force until all member states had ratified it, on 24 October 1945. This marked the official foundation of the

UN and the end of the League of Nations.

The aims and principles of the UN

The Charter of the United Nations is central to the organisation: it sets out its objectives and outlines the principles, rights and duties to be respected by all member states.

The UN has four main objectives, which are very similar to the goals of the League of Nations:

- to maintain international peace and security by encouraging friendly relations between countries;
- to ensure respect for justice, tolerance, the freedom of others, the self-determination of peoples and the defence of human rights;
- to help disadvantaged countries to improve their situation and to overcome hunger, illiteracy and illness;
- to encourage technological and social progress.

The essential principles of the organisation are listed in its Charter:

- the sovereign equality of all member states;

- the settling of international disputes by peaceful means without recourse to the threat or use of force against the territorial integrity or political independence of any state;
- the respect of peoples' right to self-determination;
- non-intervention in matters which are essentially within the domestic jurisdiction of any state.

The composition of the UN

The structure of the new organisation was based on that of the League of Nations. It comprises six main organs:

- **The General Assembly.** This is a sort of parliament for member states, and is the only organ where all the member states are represented. It carries out a wide range of activities, as it is tasked with researching, discussing and making recommendations to encourage international cooperation. However, these recommendations are not binding, so no nation is obliged to follow them. The General Assembly also elects the members of other UN organs and oversees the activities of certain organisations and agencies.

Although the General Assembly's influence is somewhat limited, it does sometimes draw attention to important issues, thus forcing the international community to take a stance or tackle serious problems, such as decolonisation in Africa and apartheid in South Africa. For decision-making purposes, each member state has one vote, regardless of its size or population, and normally a simple majority is needed. Nonetheless, for some more important issues, such as the UN's budget or the admission of a new member, a two-thirds majority in the General Assembly is needed.

- **The Security Council.** This originally comprised 11 members, five of which were permanent (the USSR, the USA, the UK, France and China) and six of which were non-permanent members elected by the General Assembly for two-year terms. As more countries joined the UN, an amendment to the Charter in 1965 increased the number of the seats on the Council to 15, with the same five permanent members and ten non-permanent members chosen in a way that ensures that each continent is fairly represented.

Controversial membership

When the UN was founded, China was represented by the USA-backed Republic of China rather than by the People's Republic of China (PRC), which was only established in 1949.

The PRC's request to join the UN, with the support of the USSR, sparked fierce debate. Between 1949 and 1971, the USA used its right to veto every time the matter was brought up in order to block the request. However, on 25 October 1971, it finally gave in so as to improve its relations with the PRC, which ended up joining the Security Council and becoming the country's only representative, as Taiwan (which by then was the only territory still governed by the Republic of China) was now excluded.

The Security Council is responsible for maintaining peace and security throughout the world, which means that it has a duty to prevent the outbreak of war. When a country at war is referred to it, the Security Council votes on a decision (known as a resolution) that all the states involved should respect. The Council acts gradually:

- When a nation lodges a complaint, it evaluates the possibility of negotiating a peaceful resolution to the conflict.
- If no peaceful solution can be found and the Council concludes that there is a serious threat to peace, or that peace has been violated, it can impose diplomatic or financial sanctions. For example, when Iraq invaded Kuwait in 1990, a blockade was imposed.
- If these measures fail to resolve the situation, the Charter allows the Security Council to send an armed contingent (the Blue Berets) to conflict zones, either to guarantee peace after the warring parties have agreed to a ceasefire, or to bring about peace when neither side is prepared to put an end to the war.

Resolutions are passed if a majority of nine of the Security Council's members vote for them, but each permanent member also has a veto which allows them to block any decisions taken by the other countries. The right to veto was a major bone of contention when the Charter was being drawn up, caused significant problems during the Cold War, and continues to hamper effective action today.

> **DID YOU KNOW?**
>
> The UN does not have its own army. The Blue Berets, the force tasked with maintaining or re-establishing peace and security around the world, is made up of military contingents from UN member states, which put personnel and material at the organisation's disposal.
>
> Their duties include ensuring that cease-fires are observed, guaranteeing respect for human rights, protecting civilians and mine-clearing. However, in some cases the Security Council may call on an international organisation that is independent of the UN, such as NATO, to carry out peacekeeping operations. At present, there are around 110 000 UN peacekeepers working on 15 operations in countries including Haiti, India, Mali, Liberia, the Democratic Republic of the Congo and the Central African Republic.

- **The Secretariat.** The UN's main management organ is appointed for renewable five-year terms. Its 9000 employees, who are based in major world cities including New York, Vienna and Geneva, are civil servants from the different member states. They carry out administrative tasks assigned by the other UN organs, prepare reports and carry out research and investigations, among other work. The Secretariat is also in charge of communicating complaints to the Security Council and informing the organisation about any threats to international security.

  The Secretariat is led by the Secretary-General, who is elected for a five-year term by the General Assembly based on a recommendation from the Security Council. The Secretary-General is both the UN's spokesperson and the public face of the institution, and is often called on to serve as chief negotiator in cases of conflict.

- **The Economic and Social Council.** This body coordinates the economic and social activities of the organisation's various programmes and encourages international cooperation with the aim of improving conditions in less developed countries. It was initially made up of 18 countries which were elected for three-year terms by the General Assembly, but since the amendments of 1965 and 1974, this number has risen to 54.

- **The Trusteeship Council.** This organ initially supervised the management of territories placed under the administration of the UN and supported them on the road to autonomy or independence. It developed out of the League of Nations' mandate system and was created to prevent the former colonies of defeated countries from being annexed by the winners. The administration of each colony was entrusted to a trustee country until its status could be determined. As the decolonisation movement gathered pace during the 1950s and 1960s, the Council's role gradually diminished until 1994, when the last country under trusteeship, Palau in the Caroline Islands, gained its independence. Since then, the Council has taken on new responsibilities, such as overseeing humanity's common heritage and creating a discussion space for minority and aboriginal peoples.
- **The International Court of Justice.** This is

the main judicial organ of the UN, and has been headquartered in The Hague since it was founded in 1946. It comprises 15 judges, representing a sample of the major international legal systems, who are elected for nine years through two separate votes, one by the General Assembly and the other by the Security Council. It provides legal opinions for the other organs upon request and can also make binding rulings, but only when the parties involved submit to its jurisdiction. In these cases, the decision must be communicated to the Security Council and monitored.

The United Nations System refers to the numerous administrative divisions in specific fields outside the organisation's six main bodies. These subsidiary organs and agencies are connected to the General Assembly or the Economic and Social Council. The best-known divisions include:

- the International Bank for Reconstruction and Development (IBRD), founded in 1945;
- the Food and Agriculture Organization (FAO), founded in 1945;
- the International Monetary Fund (IMF), founded in 1945;

- the International Labor Organization (ILO), founded in 1946;
- the World Health Organization (WHO), founded in 1946;
- the United Nations Educational, Scientific and Cultural Organization (UNESCO), founded in 1946;
- the International Atomic Energy Agency (IAEA), founded in 1956;
- the International Development Organization (IDA), founded in 1960.

IMPACT

INTERNATIONAL PEACE AND SECURITY

One of the UN's main objectives is to preserve international peace and security. During the Cold War, a first wave of interventions (a total of 13 between 1948 and 1988) took place in Africa, Asia and the Middle East.

Immediately after its creation, the UN was called on to resolve a territorial dispute between two communities triggered by the end of Great Britain's mandate over one of its colonies: Palestine, which was claimed by both Palestinians and Israelis. On 29 November 1947, the General Assembly voted to split the territory in two, thus abandoning the idea of a united state in favour of a binational federal state. In practice, this meant that an Arab state and a Jewish state would coexist, with the capital Jerusalem, which would now be classed as an international city, administered by the UN. However, the plan's failure and its consequences are well known, and the conflict is still ongoing some 70 years later. An initial peacekeeping force was sent to the region as an unarmed observer in 1948 to ensure that the truce was being respected. The Blue Berets intervened for the first time during the Suez Crisis (1956), a conflict between Egypt and a coalition comprising Israel, France and the United Kingdom following the nationalisation of the Suez Canal.

> **DID YOU KNOW?**
>
> The UN's early development took place in a particular context, namely the Cold War, which set the USSR against the USA. These two superpowers and their respective allies formed two ideologically and economically opposed blocs.
>
> The Eastern and Western blocs also faced off within the UN, giving rise to a number of disagreements. Few military measures for threats to or violations of the peace could be taken during this period, because the tensions between the USA and the USSR made it difficult for the Security Council

> to determine which one was the aggressor. Furthermore, the right to veto meant that each country could block any decisions that went against its own interests. Between 1945 and 2000, these two countries exercised their right to veto a total of 185 times. The two blocs also used the UN for their own ends during the period preceding the fall of the Berlin Wall in 1989. This means that the organisation was unable to prevent a series of hostilities (the First Indochina War, 1946-1954; the Korean War, 1950-1953; the Vietnam War, 1954-1975, the Soviet-Afghan War, 1979-1989) and crises (the Berlin Blockade in 1948 and the Suez Crisis).

Since the fall of the Berlin Wall, over 50 second-generation operations have been carried out to fulfil a range of objectives: election oversight in Cambodia (1991-1993), humanitarian aid in Somalia, the presence of Blue Berets in Cyprus, and so on. In spite of the growing number of interventions, the UN has been criticised for failing to prevent the Rwandan genocide in 1994, which resulted in almost 800 000 deaths. The UN was also heavily criticised following the Srebrenica massacre in Bosnia and Herzegovina in July 1995, as a lack of information from New York meant that the 400 Blue Berets stationed in the area did nothing to stop the killing of civilians. However, sometimes UN forces fail to intervene because one of the members of the Security Council has exercised their right to veto: for example, vetoes by China and the USSR prevented action from being taken in Tibet and Chechnya respectively. Consequently, some experts believe that the structures of the UN are poorly equipped to deal with current challenges and have proposed a complete overhaul of its administration.

DISARMAMENT AND NUCLEAR CONTROL

The founding members of the UN hoped that a sustained period of peace would mean that the quantity of armaments around the world would remain under control and decrease over the long term. Although this has clearly not been achieved, the organisation played an important role in the negotiation of numerous multilateral treaties during the Cold War, such as the Partial Nuclear Test Ban Treaty (1963), a treaty forbidding nations from sending weapons of mass destruction into orbit or placing them on the moon or any other celestial body (1966), and the Treaty on the Non-Proliferation of Nuclear Weapons (1968). That said, it was over 20 years until all the nuclear powers ratified the third of these. Similarly, the Comprehensive Nuclear-Test-Ban Treaty was adopted by the UN General Assembly in 1996, but has still not entered into force. In spite of the complexity of its missions, the UN is still trying to eliminate weapons of mass destruction and to limit and control armaments and nuclear weaponry.

SUPPORT FOR ECONOMIC WELLBEING AND COOPERATION

The UN also counts many subsidiary organisations and specialised agencies charged with promoting economic wellbeing and cooperation in fields such as postwar reconstruction, technical support, trade and development.

After the destruction wreaked during the Second World War, the UN created the International Refugee Organization (1947-1951), which assumed most of the functions of the United Nations Relief and Rehabilitation Administration (created in 1943). A range of commissions were subsequently established: one for Asia was founded in 1947, one for Latin America in 1948 and one for Africa in 1958. After the decolonisation of the 1950s and 1960, the UN set up a series of organs to tackle the issue of economic development in these countries. Furthermore, although it has no formal connection to the UN, the World Bank provides grants and subsidies to developing countries and has supported over 12 000 development projects in more than 100 countries since 1947.

SUPPORT FOR SOCIAL WELLBEING AND COOPERATION

Due to the new challenges of the late 20th century, major migratory movements and serious humanitarian crises, the UN has taken on a greater role in terms of social development and has achieved some impressive successes in improving the health and wellbeing of the global population.

Human rights

On 10 December 1948, the General Assembly adopted the Universal Declaration of Human Rights, which outlines the fundamental and natural rights of humankind as they are recognised and accepted in Western democracies. The International Covenant on Civil and Political Rights and the International Covenant on Economic, Social and Cultural Rights were both ratified in 1966, but were not signed by all member states. The UN also seeks to defend the rights of children and women, for example with the Convention on the Rights of the Child in 1989.

The environment

The UN has also taken action to tackle environmental issues. In 1972, it organised the Conference on the Human Environment in response to global concerns about environmental problems. This conference led to the creation of the United Nations Environment Programme, which was tasked with finding solutions to a range of environmental problems, including deforestation, pollution and global warming, and was responsible for the 1987 Montreal Protocol, which set out measures to protect the ozone layer.

Furthermore, the Rio de Janeiro Earth Summit in 1992 (which was followed by the United Nations Conference on Sustainable Development, also held in Rio, in 2012) was an international conference which resulted in a plan for the sustainable development of the earth's resources in the 20th century. Finally, the United Nations Framework Convention on Climate Change entered into force in 1994 and is governed by a conference of the parties which has met every year since 1995 and has achieved advances including the Kyoto Protocol in 2005, which aims to reduce greenhouse gases.

Public health and welfare

There are two major bodies linked to the United Nations that aim to improve the welfare of the global population. They are the United Nations Children's Fund (UNICEF), which was created in 1946 to respond to the needs of children in countries left devastated by the Second World War and became a part of the United Nations System in 1953. UNICEF provides humanitarian and development aid to children and vulnerable mothers: for example, it helps to feed children in over 100 countries, provides subsistence items and works to eradicate childhood diseases. As well as working to improve children's living conditions, it also has an important oversight role and ensures that their rights are respected.

The World Health Organization (WHO) works to improve the health of the world's population through activities such as vaccination campaigns in developing countries, the regulation of pharmaceutical firms to ensure that quality standards for medication are respected, interventions in epidemics and, above all, actions to combat the spread of AIDS.

Refugees

In the aftermath of the Second World War, the International Refugee Organization was tasked with repatriating, resettling and providing for the basic needs of almost a million refugees. In 1952, this organisation was replaced by the United Nations High Commissioner for Refugees (UNHRC), shortly after the signature of the 1951 Convention Relating to the Status of Refugees.

This was preceded by a more specific agency, the United Nations Relief and Works Agency for Palestine Refugees in the Near East, which was set up in 1949 to assist Palestinian populations who had settled in neighbouring states.

> **DID YOU KNOW?**
>
> The UNHRC is an apolitical humanitarian organisation which was created in 1950 and now works to help over 50 million refugees around the world. It has won the Nobel Peace Prize twice, in 1954 and 1981.

A WORLD WITHOUT THE UN

Some experts believe that the future of the UN is uncertain unless its structure and operational procedures are overhauled. Indeed, there are a number of problems stemming from the fact that the institution was created in a specific postwar context and has not evolved since, which means that it is ill-equipped to deal with contemporary problems. The main criticisms of the UN include:

- The increasing number of specialised institutions and agencies linked to the UN allegedly reduces the effectiveness of the organisation's activities. The work carried out by this multitude of international agencies often ends up overlapping and fragmenting the UN's activities.
- The organisation may not be able to effectively represent its 193 member states, as it is often torn between sometimes contradictory demands from countries which are each seeking to protect their own interests. For example, repeated vetoes by Russia and China have made it impossible to impose sanctions on Bashar al-Assad's (born in 1956) regime in Syria, and the US stance in 2011 made it impossible to criticise Israel's policy of colonisation.
- The composition of the Security Council, with its five permanent members which each have the right to veto, was established 60 years ago and is no longer suited to the current diplomatic reality. Critics point to the disproportionate power wielded by the five dominant countries and suggest increasing the number of permanent members to include new major powers, as well as reforming the right to veto so that

it can only be exercised in certain situations.
- Some of the rules in the Charter of the United Nations, such as the rule forbidding the organisation from intervening in a country until it has received the express agreement of that country, hamper its activity. For example, this rule explains the heavily-criticised delay before the UN's humanitarian intervention in Darfur in 2011.

This list is far from exhaustive, and a number of other issues have tarnished the organisation's image. For example, the UN failed to prevent the Rwandan genocide in 1994 or protect the country's Tutsi population, and when a devastating earthquake struck Haiti in 2010, the UN struggled to coordinate aid quickly, leaving the USA to lead the relief effort.

That said, the UN's many strong points are widely recognised by experts, who tend to see it as an essential instrument for international political dialogue. The UN enjoys widespread public support and serves above all as a diplomatic forum and a place for dialogue between almost all the world's countries. Its role in the development of norms and standards has been crucial in shaping the world we live in today.

SUMMARY

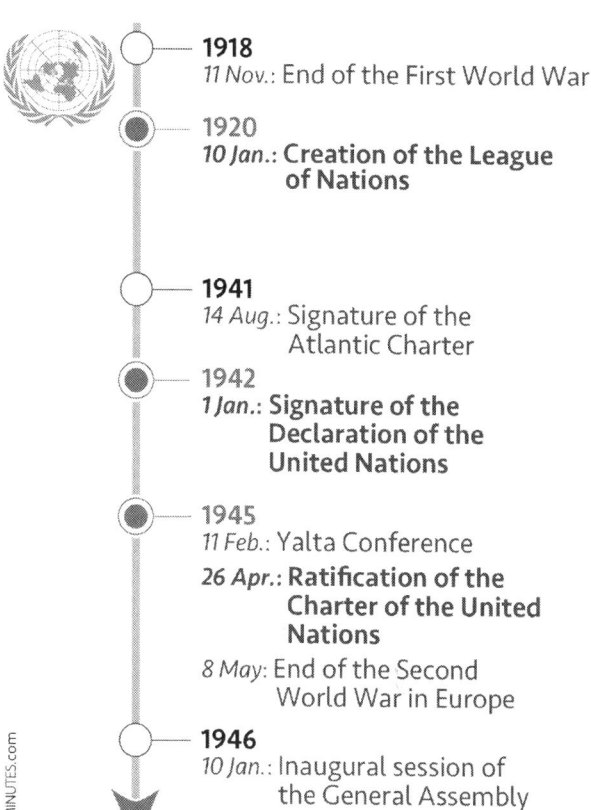

1918
11 Nov.: End of the First World War

1920
10 Jan.: **Creation of the League of Nations**

1941
14 Aug.: Signature of the Atlantic Charter

1942
1 Jan.: **Signature of the Declaration of the United Nations**

1945
11 Feb.: Yalta Conference

26 Apr.: Ratification of the Charter of the United Nations

8 May: End of the Second World War in Europe

1946
10 Jan.: Inaugural session of the General Assembly

- The League of Nations, which was founded on 10 January 1920 and initially comprised 42 member states working together to maintain peace around the world, was the forerunner of the United Nations.
- The Declaration of St. James's Palace was signed on 12 June 1941 and constituted the first step in the process leading to the creation of the UN.
- On 14 August 1941, the American president Franklin D. Roosevelt and the British prime minister Winston Churchill signed the Atlantic Charter, which established the principles behind international cooperation with the aim of maintaining peace and security.
- On 1 January 1942, representatives of the 26 countries at war against the Axis signed the Declaration of the United Nations.
- The initial plan for the UN was drawn up at the Conference of Dumbarton Oaks from 21 September to 7 October 1944. It was attended by representatives from the USSR, the USA, China and Great Britain, who discussed the institution's aims, principles, structures and functioning.
- The work begun at the Conference of

Dumbarton Oaks was completed at the Yalta Conference on 11 February 1945, which brought Franklin D. Roosevelt, Winston Churchill and Joseph Stalin together for the first time.
- On 26 April 1945, representatives from 50 countries signed the Charter of the United Nations, which had been drawn up at the San Francisco Conference.
- On 24 October 1945, the Charter of the United Nations was ratified by all the organisation's founding member states, meaning that the UN, which would be headquartered in New York, was officially created.
- The inaugural session of the General Assembly was held in London on 10 January 1946 and was attended by delegates from 51 countries. Its first resolution concerned the eradication of weapons of mass destruction, and this was followed by a series of operations with the aim of maintaining peace and the welfare of citizens on a global level.

*We want to hear from you!
Leave a comment on your online library
and share your favourite books on social media!*

FIND OUT MORE

BIBLIOGRAPHY

- Bernstein, S. and Milza, P. (2006) *Histoire du XXe siècle. Le monde entre guerre et paix. 1945-1973.* Paris: Hatier.

- Casalis, D. et al. (1976) *Histoire des États-Unis.* Paris: Larousse.

- Chaumont, C. and Mestre-Lafay, F. (2000) *L'ONU.* Paris: PUF.

- Compagnon, O. (No date) Création de l'ONU. *Encyclopædia Universalis.* [Online]. [Accessed 30 November 2017]. Available from: <https://www.universalis.fr/encyclopedie/creation-de-l-o-n-u/>

- Debouzy, M. (No date) Roosevelt, Franklin Delano (1882-1945). *Encyclopædia Universalis.* [Online]. [Accessed 30 November 2017]. Available from: <https://www.universalis.fr/encyclopedie/franklin-delano-roosevelt/>

- Fomerand, J., Lynch, C. and Mingst, K. (No date) Nations unies (ONU). *Encyclopædia Universalis.* pp. 927-937.

- Hubac, J. (2013) *Dictionnaire chronologique des guerres du XXe siècle.* Paris: Hatier.

- Tavernier, P. (1996) *Les Casques bleus*. Paris: PUF.

- The United Nations (No date) *Charter of the United Nations*. [Online]. [Accessed 4 December 2017]. Available from: <http://www.un.org/en/charter-united-nations/index.html>

- The United Nations (No date) *History of the United Nations*. [Online]. [Accessed 4 December 2017]. Available from: <http://www.un.org/en/sections/history/history-united-nations/>

- The United Nations (No date) *Homepage*. [Online]. [Accessed 4 December 2017]. Available from: <http://www.un.org/en/index.html>

- (2010) *Une autre ONU pour un autre monde*. Paris: Tribord.

ADDITIONAL SOURCES

- Annan, K. (2013) *Interventions: A Life in War and Peace*. London: Penguin.

- McWhinney, E. (1984) *United Nations Law Making: Cultural and Ideological Relativism and International Law Making for an Era of Transition*. Teaneck, New Jersey: Holms & Meier Publishers, Inc.

- Mingst, K. A. and Karns, M. P. (2011) *The United Nations in the 21st Century*. Boulder, Colorado: Westview Press.

- De Saeger, A. (2015) *The United Nations Development Programme*. Trans. Probert, C. Brussels: Plurilingua Publishing.

- Weiss, T. G. and Daws, S. eds. (2008) *The Oxford Handbook on the United Nations*. Oxford: Oxford University Press.

- Weiss, T. G., Forsythe, D. P., Coate, R. A. and Pease, K-K. (2016) *The United Nations and Changing World Politics*. Eighth edition. Boulder, Colorado: Westview Press.

ICONOGRAPHIC SOURCES

- Portrait of Franklin D. Roosevelt, dated 1933. © Elias Goldensky.

FILMS

- *Warriors*. (1999) [TV movie]. Peter Kominsky. Dir. UK: British Broadcasting Corporation, Deep Indigo Productions.

- *Hotel Rwanda*. (2004) [Film]. Terry George. Dir. UK/South Africa/Italy: United Artists.

- *Beyond the Gates*. (2005) [Film]. Michael Caton-Jones. Dir. UK/Germany: CrossDay Productions Ltd., ARTE, BBC Films, Egoli Tossell Films, Filmstiftung Nordrhein-Westfalen, Invicta Capital, UK Film Council, Zweites Deutsches Fernsehen.

- *The Whistleblower.* (2010) [Film]. Larysa Kondracki. Dir. Canada/Germany: Samuel Goldwyn Films.

50MINUTES.com

- History
- Business
- Coaching
- Book Review
- Health & Wellbeing

IMPROVE YOUR GENERAL KNOWLEDGE
IN A BLINK OF AN EYE !

www.50minutes.com

Although the editor makes every effort to verify the accuracy of the information published, 50Minutes.com accepts no responsibility for the content of this book.

© 50MINUTES.com, 2017. All rights reserved.

www.50minutes.com

Ebook EAN: 9782806289957

Paperback EAN: 9782806289964

Legal Deposit: D/2016/12603/782

Cover: © Primento

Digital conception by Primento, the digital partner of publishers.

Printed in Great Britain
by Amazon